I0829456
Belonging to :

FAMILY
Coloring Funny

FAMILY Coloring Funny

FAMILY
Coloring Funny

FAMILY
Coloring Funny

FAMILY
Coloring Funny

FAMILY Coloring Funny

FAMILY
Coloring Funny

FAMILY
Coloring Funny

FAMILY
Coloring Funny

FAMILY
Coloring Funny

FAMILY
Coloring Funny

FAMILY
Coloring Funny

FAMILY
Coloring Funny

FAMILY
Coloring Funny

FAMILY
Coloring Funny

FAMILY
Coloring Funny

FAMILY
Coloring Funny

FAMILY
Coloring Funny

FAMILY
Coloring Funny

FAMILY
Coloring Funny

FAMILY
Coloring Funny

FAMILY
Coloring Funny

FAMILY
Coloring Funny

FAMILY
Coloring Funny

FAMILY
Coloring Funny

FAMILY
Coloring Funny

FAMILY
Coloring Funny

FAMILY
Coloring Funny

FAMILY
Coloring Funny

FAMILY
Coloring Funny

FAMILY
Coloring Funny

FAMILY
Coloring Funny

FAMILY
Coloring Funny

FAMILY
Coloring Funny

FAMILY
Coloring Funny

FAMILY
Coloring Funny

FAMILY
Coloring Funny

FAMILY
Coloring Funny

FAMILY
Coloring Funny

FAMILY
Coloring Funny

FAMILY
Coloring Funny

FAMILY
Coloring Funny

FAMILY
Coloring Funny

FAMILY
Coloring Funny

FAMILY
Coloring Funny

FAMILY
Coloring Funny

FAMILY
Coloring Funny

FAMILY
Coloring Funny

FAMILY
Coloring Funny

FAMILY
Coloring Funny